Animals

Colouring book for kids

This Colouring book
Belongs to:

....

....

Try Your Colouring Pencil Before Colouring

Try Your Colouring Pencil

Before Colouring

Try Your Colouring Pencil
Before Colouring

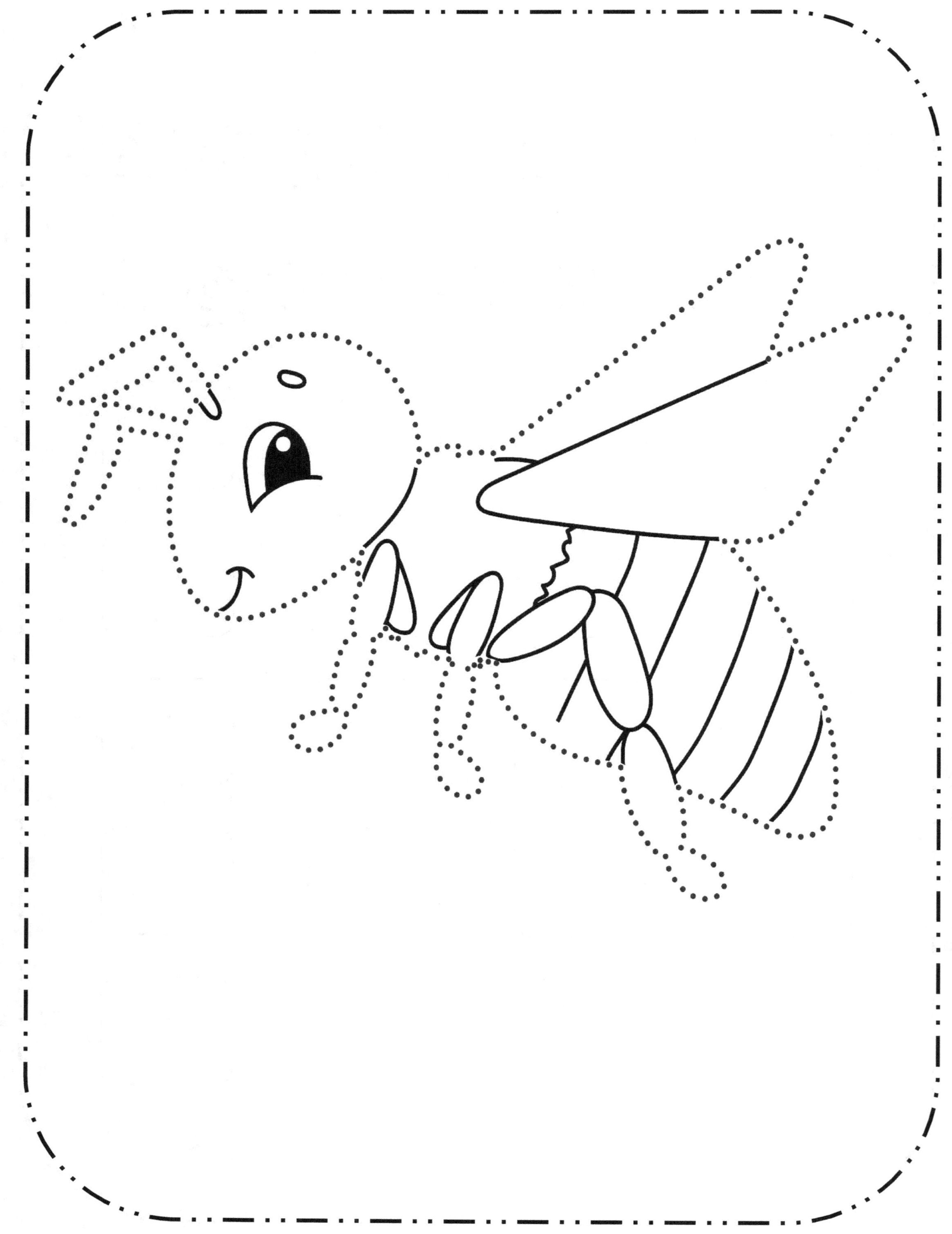

Try Your Colouring Pencil Before Colouring

Try Your Colouring Pencil Before Colouring

Try Your Colouring Pencil
Before Colouring

Try Your Colouring Pencil Before Colouring

Try Your Colouring Pencil Before Colouring

Try Your Colouring Pencil Before Colouring

Try Your Colouring Pencil Before Colouring

Try Your Colouring Pencil Before Colouring

Try Your Colouring Pencil

Before Colouring

Try Your Colouring Pencil Before Colouring

Try Your Colouring Pencil

Before Colouring

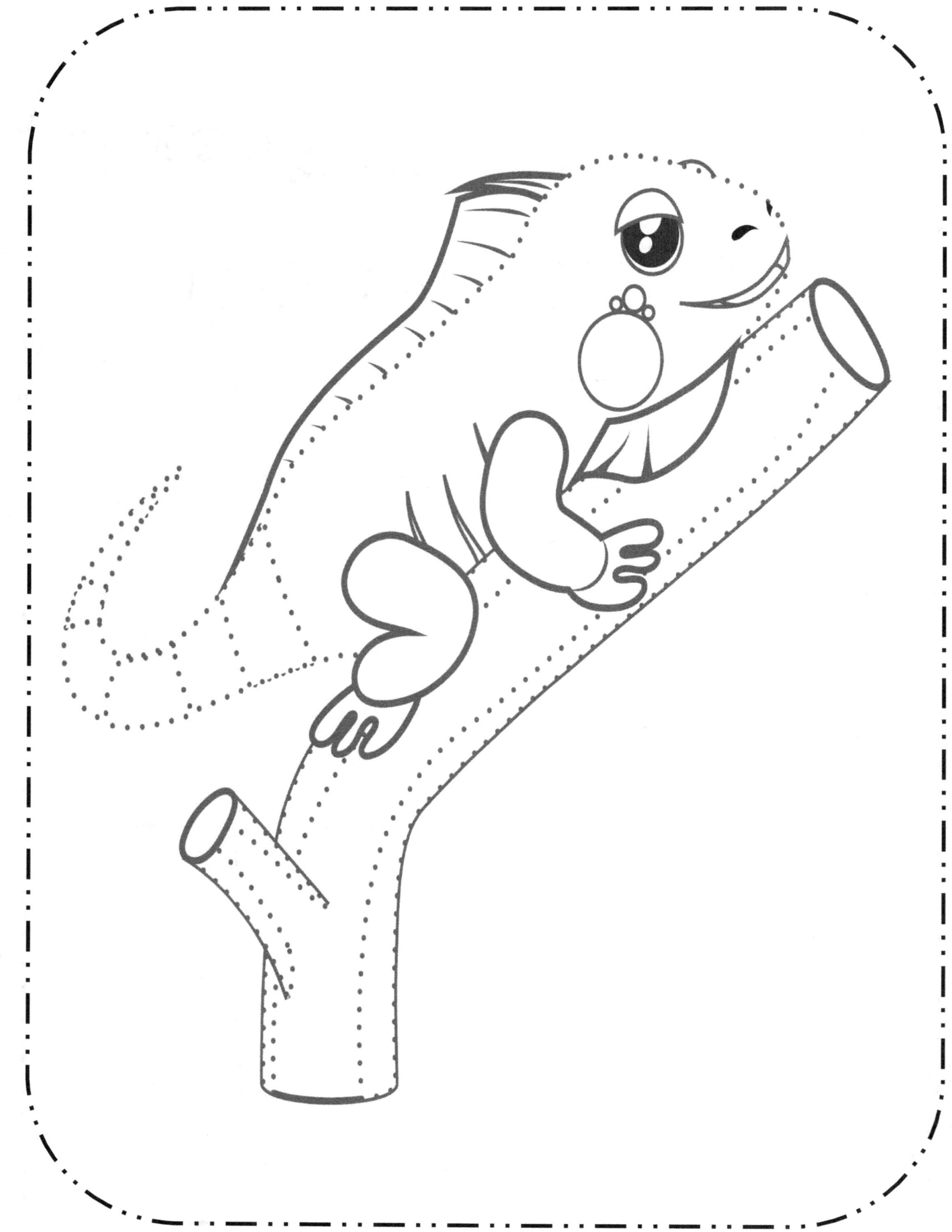

Try Your Colouring Pencil Before Colouring

Try Your Colouring Pencil

Before Colouring

Try Your Colouring Pencil Before Colouring

Try Your Colouring Pencil

Before Colouring

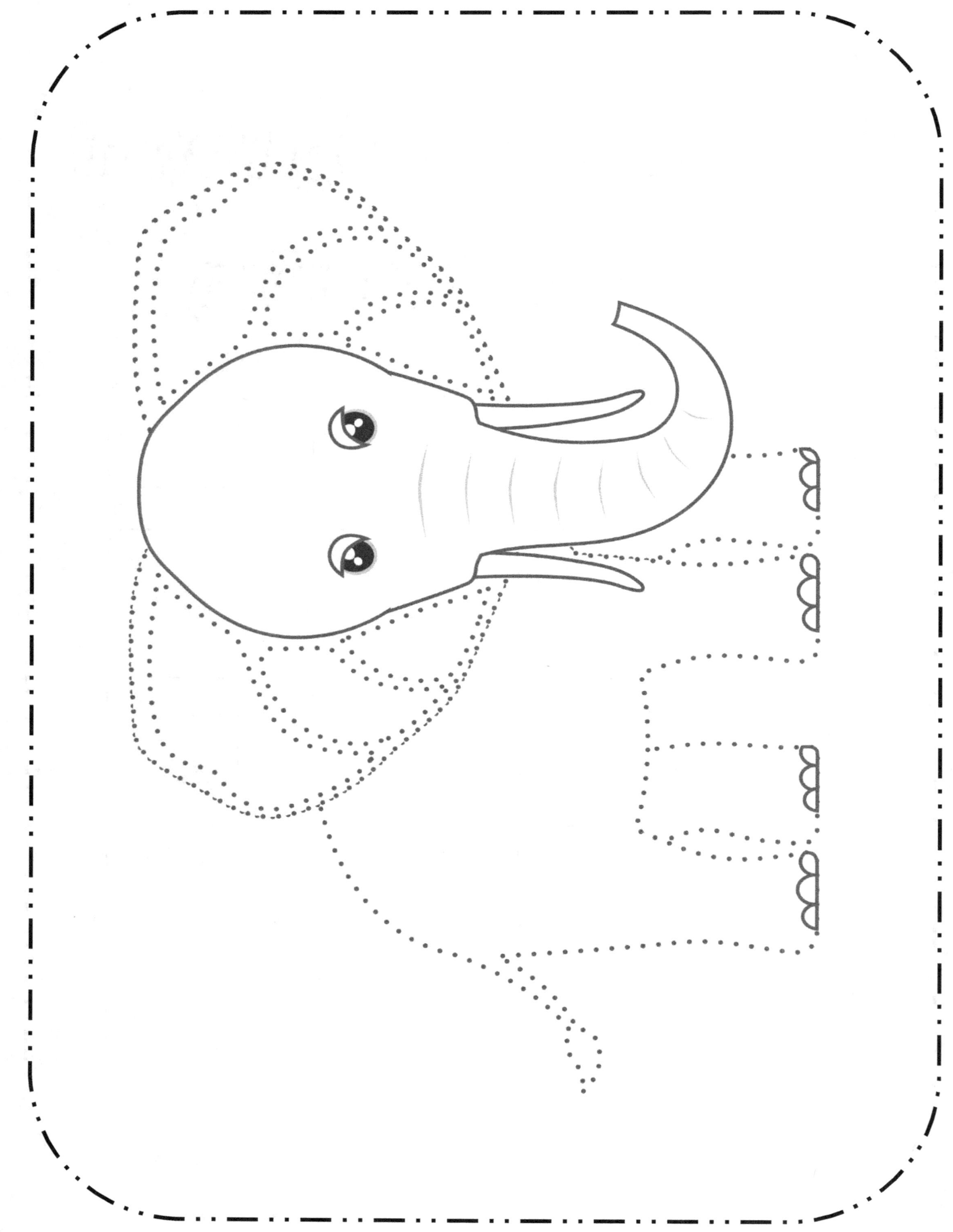

Try Your Colouring Pencil Before Colouring

Try Your Colouring Pencil

Before Colouring

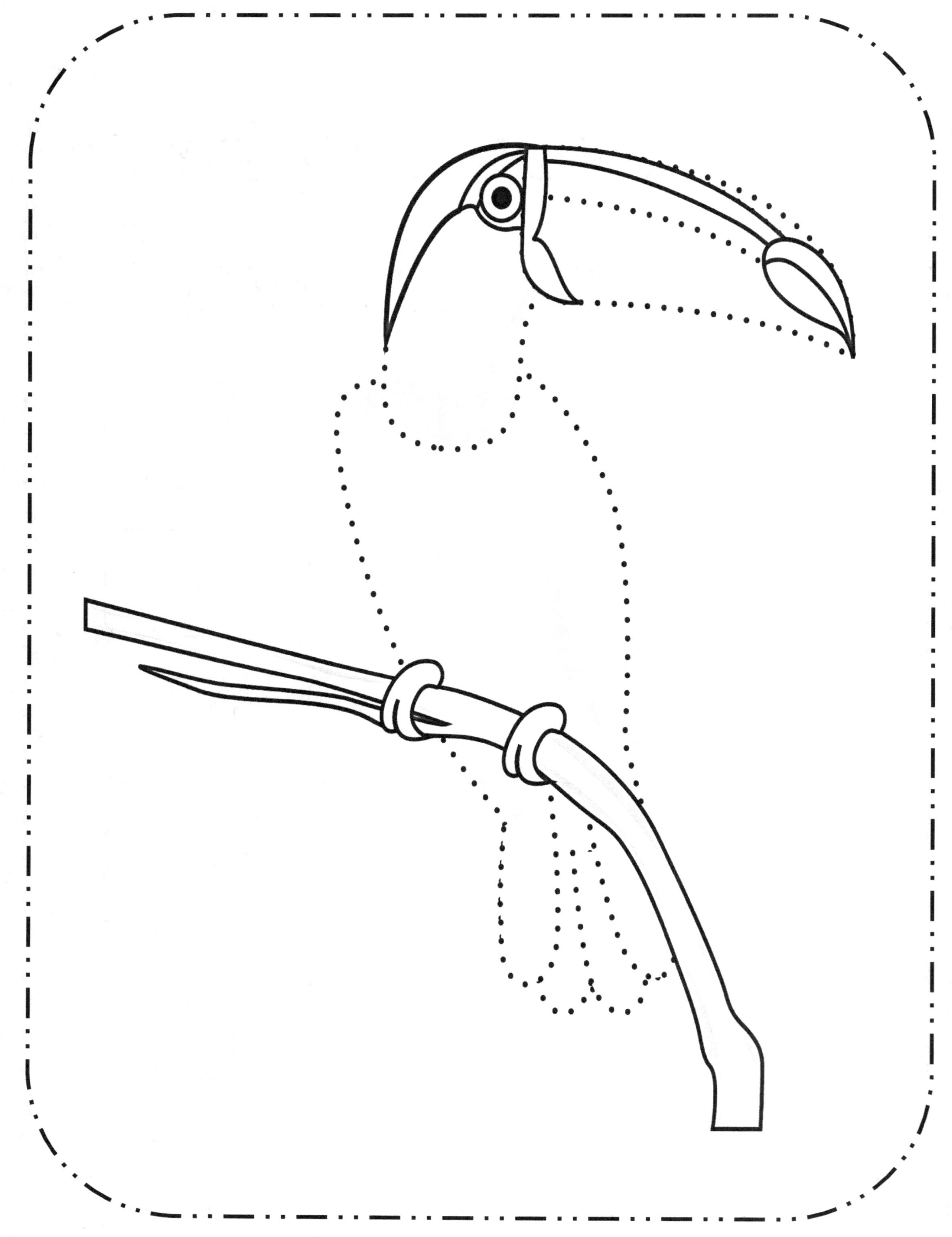

Try Your Colouring Pencil Before Colouring

Try Your Colouring Pencil Before Colouring

Try Your Colouring Pencil
Before Colouring

Try Your Colouring Pencil
Before Colouring

Try Your Colouring Pencil Before Colouring

Try Your Colouring Pencil
Before Colouring

Try Your Colouring Pencil Before Colouring

Try Your Colouring Pencil

Before Colouring

Try Your Colouring Pencil

Before Colouring

Try Your Colouring Pencil

Before Colouring

Try Your Colouring Pencil Before Colouring

Try Your Colouring Pencil Before Colouring